I0765497

How to Train Your Great Dane

An Expert Guide to Smart Socialization Strategies for Caring, Grooming, and Raising a Confident Giant Breed Dog

Finnley Crestwood

Copyright © 2024, Finnley Crestwood

All rights reserved. No part of this publication may be reproduced, distributed, or transmitted in any form or by any means, including photocopying, recording, or other electronic or mechanical methods, without the prior written permission of the publisher, except in the case of brief quotations embodied in critical reviews and certain other noncommercial uses permitted by copyright law. For permission requests, write to the publisher at the address below.

Disclaimer

The information in this book is intended for general guidance on training. It is not a substitute for professional advice. Always consult with a veterinarian or certified dog trainer for tailored recommendations. The author and publisher disclaim any liability for actions taken based on the content of this book.

Finnley Crestwood

How to Train your

Great Dane

An Expert Guide to Smart Socialization Strategies for Caring, Grooming, and Raising a Confident Giant Breed Dog

Contents

Introduction 7

Chapter One 11

Understanding the Great Dane Breed 11

Origins and History of the Breed 11

Typical Great Dane Temperament and Personality 13

Considerations for Owning a Giant Breed Dog 15

Chapter Two 17

Preparing for Your Great Dane Puppy 17

Finding a Responsible Breeder 17

Puppy-Proofing Your Home 19

Gathering Essential Supplies 22

Chapter Three 25

House Training Your Great Dane 25

Setting Up a Routine and Schedule 25

Crate Training Techniques 27

Managing Accidents Positively 29

Chapter Four   **33**

Socializing Your Great Dane Puppy   **33**

    Introducing Your Puppy to New People   33

    Getting Your Pup Used to Other Animals   35

    Exposing Your Puppy to New Environments   37

Chapter Five   **41**

Teaching Basic Cues   **41**

    Teaching Sit, Down, Stay and Come   41

    Loose Leash Walking   43

    Relaxation and Settling Cues   44

Chapter Six   **47**

Addressing Unwanted Behaviors   **47**

    Preventing and Redirecting Nipping   47

    Stopping Jumping Up   49

    Curbing Excessive Barking   51

Chapter Seven   **55**

Ongoing Training and Proofing   **55**

    Advanced obedience work   55

    Maintaining Reliability Off-Leash   60

Preparing for Therapy/Service Work   63

Chapter Eight   **67**

Meeting Your Great Dane's Needs   **67**

Providing Adequate Physical Exercise   67

Keeping Your Great Dane Mentally Stimulated
69

Managing a Giant Breed Diet   71

Chapter Nine   **75**

Health and Care for Your Great Dane   **75**

Grooming and Coat Care   75

Recognizing Common Health Issues   77

Caring for a Senior Great Dane   80

Chapter Ten   **83**

Enjoying Your Great Dane   **83**

Including Your Dog in Activities   83

Traveling with a Great Dane   85

Fun Tricks and Games   87

Chapter Eleven   **91**

Great Dane-Specific Training

Considerations   **91**

Training for Size and Strength   91

Understanding the Gentle Giant: Temperament Insights   94

Tailoring Training to Individual Personality   96

Special Bonus   **99**

20 homemade food recipes ideas for great dane with ingredients and preparation instructions   99

Introduction

When I first laid eyes on Magnus, it was an unforgettable moment. He was a towering 175 pounds, and he was nervously staring at me from behind the breeder's knees. He exuded an air of grandeur even as a stocky Great Dane puppy. Magnus had adorable features that anyone might fall in love with, from his floppy ears to his ridiculously large paws. However, a grain of uncertainty flickered at the back of my mind. Am I truly up to the challenge of nurturing this impending behemoth?

Among gigantic breeds, Great Danes have some outstanding statistics. With a weight of 120–200 pounds, males frequently reach a shoulder height of 30 inches. Typical measurements for a female are 100–130 pounds and 28 inches in height. A Great Dane's heart is so massive that it can pump approximately 40 liters of blood per minute! It weighs more than a pound! Their vast girth is both a source of their graceful grace and a training difficulty.

Despite its formidable stature, the Great Dane temperament lives up to the breed's nickname of "Gentle Giant." Friendly, patient, and loyal, Great Danes thrive when kept as indoor companions. Their exercise needs are moderate, but their intense desire for human bonding means they should not be isolated in the yard. Proper socialization and training are crucial for developing a Great Dane to their greatest potential as a loyal family member.

My worry intensified as I coaxed a squirmy Magnus into the car that first day. He instantly began biting my seats with needle-sharp puppy teeth. Tiny in the grand scheme - but so much growth yet to accomplish! I had experience handling large breeds previously, but none quite this, well...GREAT.

Over the next year, Magnus developed into the ideal Gentle Giant. But it didn't happen without diligent training and attention on my part. His puppy antics strained my patience daily. As his size soon outpaced my own, deliberate socialization to establish bombproof manners was needed. Structure, compassion, and mutual trust marked our journey together.

Now, Magnus accompanies me everywhere with his distinctive tranquility and loyalty. He fascinates strangers of all ages with his puppy-like disposition. I can trust him off-leash and among stimulating crowds because of our training foundation. When out together, we regularly draw grins and compliments on his immaculate demeanor - the finest reward!

The Great Dane has captured my heart. Their sensitivity and spirit never cease to astound me. But make no mistake, these are not beginning dogs. Their sheer size, limited lifetime, and intensive needs put them solidly in the "experienced owner only" category. However, for the appropriate individual prepared to provide the care this magnificent breed demands from puppyhood onwards, the payback is immense.

If you anticipate bright afternoons playing in the yard, languid evenings by the fire, and a buddy strolling faithfully by your side, then perhaps you and a Great Dane are meant to be. This detailed book borrows from my many years of experience living and working with these wonderful Gentle Giants. Let me take you on the exciting path of training your very own Great Dane.

Chapter One

Understanding the Great Dane Breed

Origins and History of the Breed

The Great Dane is an old breed with its origins potentially reaching back thousands of years. Images of dogs resembling the Great Dane can be seen on Egyptian antiquities from circa 3000 BC. Large boarhounds resembling the Great Dane are also described in ancient Greek writings. While their specific origins are debatable, most experts think that the Great Dane breed as we know it today was developed in Germany by mixing the old English Mastiff with Irish Wolfhounds and Greyhounds.

The name "Great Dane" first appeared in literature in the 17th century, though the Germans referred to them as Kammerhunde or "Chamber Dogs" since they were typically kept as court companions and estate guardians. Despite their intimidating size, these canines were kept as gentle pets and revered for their devoted loyalty. Great Danes were more popular across Europe in the 18th century. The breed made its way to the US in the late 19th century and the American Kennel Club recognized its first Great Dane in 1887.

Over the decades, Great Danes have been bred largely as companion animals and show dogs. Their imposing size and care requirements make them unsuited for a more severe activity like hunting or lengthy outdoor employment. Dedicated breeding procedures have maintained the Great Dane as a loyal, dignified but playful companion. While initially bred in several color patterns, today's Great Danes are recognized in six display colors: brindle, fawn, blue, black, harlequin, and mantle. Great

Danes remain a popular companion breed globally today.

Typical Great Dane Temperament and Personality

The average Great Dane's attitude is defined as amiable, patient, dependable, and loyal. Despite their gigantic size, Great Danes are renowned as "gentle giants" and make ideal family pets when properly trained and socialized.

Great Danes are normally peaceful and easy going inside. They have relatively modest activity needs for a big breed and are fine with a couple of gentle walks per day. Given their sensitive temperament and need to be near their people, Great Danes should reside inside. They should never be isolated outside or kenneled for long periods.

Great Danes attach strongly to their families. They prefer to get along nicely with youngsters, other canines, and pets when properly introduced. Owners do need to monitor play interactions due to their huge size. While Great Danes never demonstrate significant hostility, their frightening look might make strangers nervous. Extensive socializing is essential to minimize any wariness around new people.

While highly sensitive, Great Danes are also independent thinkers capable of becoming stubborn. Positive reinforcement training is generally recommended from puppyhood on. Overall, Great Danes thrive on mild leadership, companionship, and inclusion in family activities. Their peaceful loyalty makes them great lifelong companions when given the care their huge size deserves.

Considerations for Owning a Giant Breed Dog

Great Danes are certainly a gigantic breed, with males reaching over 30 inches tall and weighing 120-200 lbs. Caring for their large bodies comes with unique considerations. Prospective owners must think through the reality before committing to one of these gentle giants.

One significant aspect is the expense. Everything is more expensive with huge breed dogs - food, meds, supplies, etc. Great Danes are prone to various health disorders like stomach torsion that may require pricey surgical therapy. Owners should have reserves to meet unanticipated vet needs.

Great Danes also need lots of space. They demand properly sized housing with room to move about and lie comfortably. Outdoor areas should have robust fencing that can contain a really large dog.

Their size makes travel and boarding problematic as well.

Giant breeds have shorter lifespans, usually only living 6-10 years. Owners must be prepared for the emotional and financial commitment of caring for a senior Great Dane and the inevitability of losing them sooner rather than later.

Training and thorough socializing are vital for producing a well-adjusted Great Dane. Owners must be prepared to put in this labor from a young age. Great Danes do best with experienced dog owners who can handle their size and sensitivities. For the appropriate owner, the Great Dane's loving devotion is tremendously rewarding. But their requirements and limited lifetime must be seriously considered.

Chapter Two

Preparing for Your Great Dane Puppy

Finding a Responsible Breeder

Finding a trustworthy, reliable breeder is crucial when getting a Great Dane puppy. Take time investigating breeders and be aware of those who appear to be running puppy mills or breeding dogs without consideration for health and temperament.

A responsible Great Dane breeder will:

- Have a selective breeding program focusing on health and temperament, not large-volume puppy production. They should breed seldom, with just 1-2 litters per year.

- Do extensive health testing on all breeding dogs for conditions including hip dysplasia, heart difficulties, thyroid disorders, etc. They should be able to produce documents.

- Breed only dogs who are 2 years old or older once growth plates have closed and health is certified.

- Carefully screen potential buyers with inquiries about the experience, lifestyle, home environment, etc. They want to ensure pups are going to excellent homes.

- Provide evidence of deworming, immunizations, and veterinarian checkups demonstrating the pups are healthy. The mother dog should also be in good shape after whelping.

- Be able to discuss the genetic history of both parents and what qualities they expect in the puppies. They should know the lineage well.

- Have a contract including things like spay/neuter, and return policy if complications arise. An excellent breeder cares about dogs for life.

Avoid breeders who seem focused on money above puppy welfare or who do not ask inquiries about your home. Be aware of "rare color" breeding or any gimmicks. Visit the breeder in person and evaluate the circumstances. A responsible breeder will welcome questions and desire the best for their Great Danes.

Puppy-Proofing Your Home

Before bringing home a Great Dane puppy, take time to completely puppy-proof your home. Their large size and hyperactive puppy energy means you'll need to keep your home safe and secure.

- Remove any minor choking risks like coins, pearls, and buttons where the puppy can reach.

- Keep appliance wires, dangerous cleaning supplies, and prescriptions carefully stored away in cupboards. Use kid locks if needed.

- Set up a confinement area utilizing a crate or puppy pen where the pup can stay when you're not home. Stock it with toys.

- Designate a place such as a laundry room for housetraining. Cover the floor with pee pads coated with newspaper.

- Buy and carefully set up a strong crate with bedding that will be large enough for an adult Great Dane.

- Remove any unstable rickety furniture or décor pieces that the pooch could knock over or pull down.

- Keep waste bins securely covered or out of reach - pups love to investigate!

- Keep shoes, vital documents, and valuables safely secured away from the puppy.

- Pick up any small items like kids' toys, pin cushions, etc. that could be swallowed.

- Cover electrical outlets and block off any dangerous places like balconies or pools.

- Install baby gates for shutting off sections as needed. Make sure they are extra tall for Danes.

- Ensure your outdoor space is entirely contained with a high fence to contain an adventurous Dane pup.

Take a crawl through your home at puppy level to uncover any other risks needing remedy before your

Great Dane arrives! Better to be puppy-proof now than risk harm later.

Gathering Essential Supplies

Once you've ready your home, establish a list of all the important materials your Great Dane puppy will need. Gather everything before pickup day so you're set for your pup's arrival.

Supplies Needed:

- Premium quality puppy kibble and treats
- Stainless steel bowls for food and water - Soft snacks for training - Sturdy leash and collar with ID tag - Brushes for grooming - Nail clippers - Dog shampoo
- Interactive chew toys of all textures
- Variety of balls, ropes, plush toys
- Dog bed and blankets

- Enzyme cleaner for accidents

- Poop sacks

- Puppy pads

- Newspaper and paper towels

- Baby gates - Exercise pen - Sturdy crate big enough for an adult dog

- Non-tippable food and water bowls

- Slow-feed dog bowl

- Car harness restraint - Dog first aid kit - Dog car hammock or cover

Having all needed items ready in advance means you can focus totally on your new dog without any annoying trips to the pet store. Shop around for savings and get quality goods that will last through puppyhood into your dog's adult life.

Chapter Three

House Training Your Great Dane

Setting Up a Routine and Schedule

House training a Great Dane puppy entails following a consistent program right from the start. Puppies thrive on regular schedules for eating, pottying, playing, and sleeping.

Establish designated potty times, ideally after meals, naps, and active play. Take your animal to their preferred potty spot and use a cue like "Go potty." Wait patiently till they go then praise and treat. Stick to this routine.

Feed your puppy on a regular schedule, 2-3 times per day. Potty them immediately after eating. Limit access to meals at least 2 hours before bedtime.

Track when they are likely to have bowel motions after eating.

Enforce nap times in the crate after play and meals. Puppies need 18-20 hours of sleep daily. Enforced naps reduce accidents and overstimulation.

Restrict access to portions of your home until consistently potty trained. Tether your dog close to you when they can't be confined. Watch for any signs they need to go.

Keep charts detailing when your pup eats, drinks, naps, plays, and potty. Look for patterns their body has established. This allows you to estimate restroom needs and prevent accidents.

Be patient! Puppies don't have full bladder and bowel control until roughly 6 months old. Stick to routines and frequently take them out. Consistency and time are crucial for house training huge breed puppies.

Crate Training Techniques

Using a crate is tremendously helpful for house training your Great Dane puppy. The crate gives a location where they can sleep, nap, and learn to "hold it." Follow these guidelines for effective crate training:

- Introduce the crate favorably from day one. Scatter snacks and toys inside so they associate it with nice things.

- Start cautiously with brief, supervised crating sessions. Reward calm behavior in the crate.

- Feed your pooch its food inside the crate to develop pleasant connections.

- Provide cozy bedding and safe chew toys in the kennel at all times.

- Use an adequately sized crate so your Dane can stand, lie down, and turn around.

- Place the crate in a heavy circulation family area so your pooch doesn't feel secluded.

- Stick to a routine with regular 1-2 hour crating sessions throughout the day.

- Take your puppy outside shortly before and after crating for potty breaks.

- Ignore minor fussing. If they escalate into panicking, never release them when working up.

- Make crate time to relax by giving stuffed Kongs or safe chews.

- Always take your pup outside immediately when released from the box.

With good introductions and constant scheduling, crate training gives the consistency puppies need to develop bladder control.

Managing Accidents Positively

Potty training is a dirty procedure! Even with constant supervision and procedures, your Great Dane puppy may inevitably have occasional indoor accidents. Stay positive when managing mistakes.

- Interrupt accidents swiftly with a calm "ah ah!" Do not penalize or scare your puppy after the incident. Just quietly interrupt then escort them outside immediately to finish.

- Thoroughly clean all messes with an enzymatic pet cleaner to remove odors they may be drawn to.

- Avoid employing severe penalties like rubbing their nose in it or yelling. This simply encourages them to dread you.

- Monitor closely and take your pooch out more frequently. Look for trends suggesting when they most need to go.

- Be patient and understanding! Puppies don't fully grasp training straight away as bladders are still maturing.

- Increase supervision and confinement when you can't actively watch. Keep them on a leash indoors if needed.

- Double-check for any medical issues if you detect excessive drinking, urination, or other strange signs.

- Stay cheerful and focused! Consistency is crucial. With time and good enforcement, your puppy will get there. Celebrate all successes.

Accidents are part of the process. Respond calmly and just get back on track. Consistent positive practices will help your Great Dane puppy establish bladder control.

Chapter Four

Socializing Your Great Dane Puppy

Introducing Your Puppy to New People

Early socialization is vital for creating a confident, pleasant Great Dane. Puppies go through a prime "socialization window" up to 14-16 weeks old. Use this opportunity to safely introduce them to many new individuals.

- Invite friends over regularly starting a few days after bringing your dog home once they're comfortable in your home. Have people offer food and pets while your pup is in your lap.

- Sign your puppy up for "puppy preschool" group programs for supervised play and training around other dogs and people. Select classes requiring immunization records.

- Ask diverse types of individuals including males, children, elderly, etc. to kneel and offer snacks to your pup when out and about. Go slowly allowing your puppy to warm up at their speed.

- Avoid pressing interactions with plainly frightened or shy puppies. Seek help from a trainer to build up their confidence using desensitization techniques.

- Take your dog frequently to packed outdoor public locations like parks where they'll observe people and city sounds. Watch for overstimulation.

- When adult dogs or vaccinated puppies visit your home, oversee all interactions but allow mutual interest and play. Correct any overzealous behavior.

- Sign up your puppy for a general handling class to teach them to accept being stroked, brushed, and examined by strangers. Reward toleration.

- Socialization is about pleasant associations. Be your pup's advocate and don't overload them with too much too quickly. Let them grow confidence at their developing speed.

Getting Your Pup Used to Other Animals

Socialization should also involve supervised exposure to other animals to prevent reactivity difficulties later on. Take these steps:

- Arrange supervised meets with friendly adult dogs belonging to family and friends. Monitor play and prevent bullying.

- Visit pet stores, dog parks, and other controlled locations to view other animals from a modest distance at first. Stay far enough away to prevent overstimulation. Reward calm behavior.

- If you have resident pets at home, supervise all interactions thoroughly. Use baby gates to develop secure zones and introduction rituals.

- Expose your dog to livestock like horses or cows if feasible. This educates them not to chase large animals. Always keep your pup leashed with cattle.

- Ask friends with puppies or mild-mannered adult dogs to join your puppy preschool programs for social time. Select balanced trainers who supervise appropriate play.

- Avoid dog parks until your Great Dane puppy is older, has complete vaccinations, and dependably listens to obedience cues. Bad situations might arise at dog parks when pups are too young.

- Cats and other tiny pets at home need safe rooms and vertical areas where they can escape an excited large dog. Use gates and leashes to manage encounters.

- Socialization is about developing positive associations through rewards and patience. Never force encounters that frighten your pup. Seek help from trainers on addressing challenges.

Exposing Your Puppy to New Environments

An important component of socialization is gradually introducing your Great Dane puppy to a wide variety of surroundings to establish confidence.

- Carry or organize transit for young puppies to discover new places including parks, stores, hikes, and cafes from the secure comfort of your arms or a stroller.

- Invite vaccinated puppies on trips like boat rides, outdoor dining, athletic events, and community occurrences to encounter new sights, sounds, and smells in a favorable light.

- Sign up for a formal "puppy walking group" program where pups follow basic obedience cues while exploring new locations each week. Always bring tempting treats on outings to promote desired conduct.

- Introduce your puppy to car journeys early on to prevent travel anxiety. Use locked boxes and start with very short journeys to fun destinations.

- Help your dog feel comfortable on varied surfaces like sidewalks, gravel, puddles, and metal grates. Lure with food while letting them approach at their speed.

- Avoid forcing your pet into frightening circumstances like packed noisy clubs or firework displays. Go slowly at their developmental stage.

- Focus on boosting your puppy's confidence by allowing them to explore new areas at their own pace while you provide praise, treats, and comfort.

- Seek locations appropriate to your lifestyle like hiking trails, packed stadiums, airports, or metro stations. Make new encounters positive.

- Well-socialized Great Danes adapt readily to new conditions later in life. Take advantage of the fragile socialization window to gently introduce your youngster to the world!

Chapter Five

Teaching Basic Cues

Teaching Sit, Down, Stay and Come

Mastering fundamental obedience cues allows you to control and bond with your Great Dane. Start teaching carefully using positive reinforcement strategies right from the start:

Sit - Hold a reward at their nose level and slowly move it over their head until their butt hits the ground as they gaze up to follow the treat. Praise and reward. Repeat "sit" each time.

Down - Ask for a seat first. Hold a treat in your fist in front of their nose. Slowly lower your fist to the floor so they follow into a down position. Reward. Say "down" as they lower.

Stay - Ask for a seat. Say "stay", take a step back, then return and reward. Gradually increase distance and duration. Reward every success.

Come - Call your puppy's name enthusiastically and sprint backward encouraging them to chase you for a treat and praise. Increase distance with time. Reward every success.

Use high-value rewards and regular repetition in short sessions. Increase requirements gradually in diverse circumstances. Remain optimistic - make it a fun game for your pup!

Practice solid cue responses utilizing long leads in safe enclosed places first before going off-leash. Proof instructions in distracting surroundings once mastered at home. Great Danes take time to dependably recall - be patient and consistent.

Loose Leash Walking

Teaching slack leash walking minimizes pulling which could be problematic with a big breed:

- Fit your Great Dane puppy with a properly fitted head collar and lightweight leash that provides you control while minimizing pain.

- Reward your puppy for focusing on you and strolling by your side. Use very high-value goodies.

- Stop quickly if they forge ahead, and change direction till the leash is loose again.

- Practice in low distraction areas first, then enhance criterion by introducing additional distractions slowly as skills grow.

- Discourage pushing forward by switching directions often using rewards to lead your pooch back to your side. Make it a game!

- If your puppy pulls frequently, pause and call them back to your side repeatedly before continuing movement. They can't pull if not moving forward.

- Avoid harsh leash corrections that may startle your pet - use positive reinforcement to shape loose leash habits.

- Consistency and time are crucial to perfecting loose leash walking. Make it easy at the beginning and applaud modest successes.

Relaxation and Settling Cues

Great Danes flourish when taught relaxation cues:

- Use goodies to encourage and reward desired behaviors like laying on their bed or mat for lengthy intervals.

- Add verbal signals like "settle" and "enough" while they are in relaxed postures so the phrases become connected.

- Practice having your Great Dane hold "stays" for increasing durations of time during their daily routine.

- Reward calm behavior in the family, use indicators like "enough" to redirect over-excitement. Manage energy levels.

- Provide adequate chews when crated or resting locations to occupy them. Kongs loaded with frozen food provide brain activity.

- Ensure your Great Dane gets appropriate physical and mental exercise to minimize destructive tendencies or unrest from boredom. A tired Dane is a well-behaved Dane!

- If your Great Dane has problems settling, get help from skilled professionals for managing any separation distress or anxiety issues.

Relaxation is an acquired skill for many canines. Put time into reinforcing serenity and impulse control. This provides a superb family companion.

Chapter Six

Addressing Unwanted Behaviors

Preventing and Redirecting Nipping

It's natural for Great Dane puppies to mouth and nip during play. Redirect this behavior consistently to minimize unpleasant mouthing:

- Provide plenty of acceptable chew toys and praise when used. Rotate the toy selection to keep it interesting.

- Avoid rough, wrestling-type play that riles up the puppy. This leads to harder mouthing.

- Teach gentle play by rewarding your puppy for licking or nuzzling instead of nipping during encounters.

- Say "ouch!" in a high-pitched tone when nipped then instantly redirect to a toy. Praise if they switch to the toy.

- Stand up and walk away if the nipping continues, halting all play for 15-30 seconds. Repeat this time out consistently each time.

- Avoid scolding or physical punishment which can make mouthing worse. Simply withdraw attention.

- Monitor children's play and separate them if the dog gets too eager and snappy.

- Provide appropriate physical and mental stimulation to prevent overtired hyperactivity that leads to nipping.

- Seek help from a trainer if your Great Dane puppy continues nipping when the new adult teeth come in at approximately 6 months old.

With patient positive reinforcement and retraining, you can curb mouthing throughout the puppy teething phase. Proper exercise and chew toys are crucial.

Stopping Jumping Up

Great Danes can inflict injuries when jumping on people. Curb this habit early on:

- Reward all four paws on the floor with food and praise. Ask for a seat when greeting.

- Avoid physically disciplining or kneeing your Great Dane, as this might make them hand-shy.

- Turn and walk away from your dog when they jump, folding your arms and ignoring them till you are relaxed. Only provide attention when all four paws are on the floor.

- Practice having guests turn away when jumped on. No one should reward jumping by interacting.

- Teach an alternative behavior when excited, such as fetching a toy on command. Redirect that energy.

- Avoid patting your Great Dane above the shoulders when greeting, since this encourages rearing up. Pet beneath the chin instead.

- Improve impulse control with remaining training and "off" cues when feet are on objects like furniture.

- Use baby gates to limit access during greetings if needed. Only allow contact while your Great Dane is calm.

- Reward desired greetings consistently over time and jumping will diminish. But you must ensure the behavior is never promoted by attention.

With positive training and vigilant family members, your Great Dane may learn to keep those giant paws on the floor!

Curbing Excessive Barking

Great Danes normally don't bark excessively. But vocal demands for attention, barking at sights/sounds, or separation anxiety might provoke problem barking:

- Ensure your Great Dane gets appropriate physical and mental exercise daily to minimize boredom and dissatisfaction.

- Provide stimulating food toys like frozen Kongs to entertain them while left alone.

- Teach "quiet" by rewarding them when they stop barking on command. Praise as soon as barking ceases. Gradually shape greater calm intervals.

- Avoid yelling or physical punishment, which might foster the barking tendency. Remain calm.

- Teach an alternative behavior instead like "go to your mat" to redirect them from barking triggers. Reward when obeyed.

- Rule out separation anxiety, fearfulness, medical difficulties, or other causes if barking remains excessive despite training. Seek expert help.

- Use noise interrupters like PetCorrector compressed air blasted at the ground to divert vocalizations. Never spray straight at your dog!

- Desensitize Great Danes to barking triggers like passing dogs or people by rewarding calm conduct in their presence.

- Crate the train to create a safe location for your Great Dane when left home alone. Cover the crate if barking is prompted by visuals.

While some vocalization is normal, excessive barking must be addressed. Maintaining an enriched schedule, practicing impulse control, and ensuring needs are satisfied will help significantly.

Chapter Seven

Ongoing Training and Proofing

Advanced obedience work

Once your dog has mastered fundamental cues like sit, stay, down, come, loose leash walking, and leaving objects alone, it's time to challenge their brains and improve your bond with advanced obedience training. Advancing your dog's education keeps them stimulated and assures a well-behaved companion in every setting.

Heelwork

Basic heelwork means your dog can walk smoothly on a loose leash by your side. Advanced heelwork demands their continuous focus and participation with you. Work on the following:

- Heeling off leash in distraction-free areas before building duration. Use high-value snacks to sustain attention.

- Gradually add distractions like toys on the ground or other people. Proof of reliability even when interesting things call your dog away from you.

- Practice quick pace changes, zig-zag patterns, sudden turns, and slow drawn-out healing. This challenges your dog's ability to pay attention.

- Expect and reward eye contact regularly. Healing is pointless if your dog is blowing you off and scanning the environment instead of monitoring you.

Hand Signals

Hand signals are crucial once the distraction level is high enough that your dog may not hear vocal cues. Reinforce obedience to the following:

- Down hand signal - sweeping flat hand toward the earth.

- Sit hand signal - upwards sweeping motion with your hand.

- Stay hand signal - open flat palm held out in stop signal.

- Come hand signal - sweeping hand toward your body.

Always reward obedience with a treat. Phase out the verbal cue progressively after the hand gesture alone elicits a dependable response.

Out-of-Sight Down Stays

A real down stay requires your dog to remain settled in place without you present. Practice:

- Leaving your dog in a down stay while you step behind a tree or corner for a few seconds before returning and praising.

- Gradually increase your out-of-sight duration. If your dog breaks the stay, go back to shorter intervals they can succeed with.

- Randomize the period you're out of sight so it's unpredictable. Gotta stay put until you return!

This difficult obedience ability demands significant discipline and impulse control from your dog. A dog capable of staying despite enticing diversions and with their owner out of sight has attained excellent training heights!

Public Access Skills

If you wish to bring your dog out in public to cafés, shops, and crowds confidently, ensure they have polished manners:

- Practice "place" commands, having your dog go to their mat or bed in busy situations. Reward quiet settling among the commotion.

- Shape loose leash strolling through crowded sidewalks, ignoring food on the ground, dismissing other dogs.

- Teach them to sit or lie down for petting from courteous strangers if you allow this. Do not let them jump up!

- Work on honing their elimination behaviors - going potty quickly on demand and not crouching every five feet during a walk!

- Desensitize to sounds and settings kids may experience such as clanging dishes, wheelchairs, and loud machines. You want nothing to surprise them.

Public access skills allow you to enjoy having your dog along for the voyage! But remember, this privilege might be removed if they demonstrate terrible manners. Maintain these talents with practice.

The beautiful thing about advanced training is you can constantly add new difficulties to keep your dog's mind engaged. Whether aiming for therapy dog certification or just a better companion, continue expanding your dog's education throughout life! The rewards of an expertly trained dog are great.

Maintaining Reliability Off-Leash

Great Danes require rigorous training to acquire off-leash rights. Never think your huge breed can go off-leash securely without proofing:

- Work up very gradually to off-leash freedom. Start in securely gated locations with no big distractions.

- Maintain a recall success rate of at least 90% before eliminating your long line. If your Great Dane fails to recall many times, go back to restraining devices.

- Always reward recalls, even if they were late coming when called. Never reprimand your Great Dane for coming to you, no matter how slowly. You want them to view coming as a positive thing.

- Practice emergency "down" cues from a distance so you can get control if needed when off-leash. Reward conformity promptly.

- Avoid off-leash privileges in unfenced, high-risk locations. Even well-trained dogs can make blunders if sufficiently afraid or preoccupied. Better safe than sorry.

- Consider a GPS monitoring collar gadget for enhanced protection if your Great Dane has good recall but you want that extra peace of mind during rural off-leash treks.

- Carry high-value incentives on all off-leash outings to emphasize cooperation. Hungry dogs listen better!

- Work consistently on involvement and obedience. Off-leash freedom is earned via training it - not a granted right. Follow norms and regulations in public locations.

With extensive proofing, you can securely enjoy off-leash excursions with your big breed. But never take their remembrance for granted. Be a responsible owner.

Preparing for Therapy/Service Work

Great Danes often thrive in therapy work and some may succeed as assistance dogs with sufficient preparation:

- Start training and socialization early to ensure great manners and bombproof temperament in public settings.

- Thorough obedience training utilizing positive ways. Great Danes undertaking therapeutic or service work must have strong obedience to vocal cues and hand signs in all circumstances.

- Habituate your Great Dane extensively to medical equipment, crowded corridors, tight places, loud unpredictable sounds, uneven balance, etc. to prepare them for healthcare facility visits. Work with experienced trainers on effective desensitization.

- Arrange for your Great Dane to earn their AKC Canine Good Citizen certification as a prerequisite for therapy dog registration.

- For service jobs, speak with professionals on training advanced disability assistance duties specific to your needs. Be realistic about what your specific Great Dane is capable of.

- Focus on public access skills like ignoring other people, strolling through crowds, eliminating on cue, and remaining unflappable amid greetings and handling from strangers.

- Arrange supervised hospital or assisted living visits to examine your Great Dane's comfort and reactivity to weak, unstable folks and medical equipment sounds.

- For service work, do public access tests exposing your Great Dane to tough settings while tasking.

Seek trainer advice to strengthen any shortcomings noted.

With devotion and adequate preparation, many Great Danes flourish in therapeutic roles or as service dogs for those in need. It is deeply gratifying work for the appropriate canine!

Chapter Eight

Meeting Your Great Dane's Needs

Providing Adequate Physical Exercise

Great Danes require daily physical exercise to preserve their health, however less than many active breeds. Focus on moderate activities appropriate for a growing gigantic breed:

- Take Great Dane puppies on short leash walks of 5-10 minutes, adding a few minutes more each week as they mature. Avoid high-impact exercise while joints are growing.

- Engage adult Danes in at least 30-60 minutes of daily exercise such as brisk walking, hiking, swimming, or jogging beside a bike. Avoid repetitive actions like stair climbing.

- Play fetch games in safe confined locations. Use balls and toys sized for a large breed to prevent choking concerns.

- Great Danes enjoy obstacle courses! Set up ramps, tunnels, fitness hurdles, etc. in your backyard for mental and physical stimulation.

- Sign up for training sessions like nose work and agility fundamentals to provide cerebral stimulation along with mild physical activity.

- Monitor Great Danes regularly for overheating and tiredness. Provide cooldowns and drink breaks. Don't over-exercise them in hot or humid weather.

- Avoid strong repetitive impacts like leaping until growth plates have closed approximately 18-24 months old.

- Require rest breaks. Great Danes are prone to injury if pushed too aggressively. Appropriate exercise for a giant breed is all about MODERATION.

- Ensure your Great Dane maintains a lean, fit body condition. Carrying excess weight places dangerous strain on already stressed joints.

Keeping Your Great Dane Mentally Stimulated

In addition to physical exercise, be sure to stimulate your Great Dane's active mind:

- Provide interactive puzzle toys that can be filled with food for your dog to manipulate and work for. Kongs, treat balls, snuffle mats etc.

- Play hide-and-seek games with toys and treats around your home and backyard. Make your dog work to find them!

- Train short sessions of new commands, tricks, and behaviors daily to exercise their brain. Great Danes love to learn.

- Offer chews like bully sticks, raw bones, and frozen stuffed Kongs to settle and occupy your dog for hours. Supervise to prevent choking.

- Take your Great Dane on outings to new locations and let them watch the world go by from parks, cafes, etc. Exposure stimulates their curious nature.

- Rotate a variety of food-dispensing and interactive toys to prevent boredom. Keep your dog guessing!

- Scatter your Great Dane's kibble around the house or yard and have them hunt for their meals rather than eat from a bowl.

- Sign up for dog sports training like nose work, rally obedience, barn hunt, etc. if your schedule permits. The mental challenge will tire out their brain.

- Provide plenty of social interactions with new friendly dogs and people frequently. Great Danes thrive on companionship.

Managing a Giant Breed Diet

Great Danes have unique nutritional needs to support their rapid growth and massive size:

- Feed high-quality large-breed puppy food for the first 12-18 months to support joint & brain development. Gradually transition to adult food.

- Follow feeding guidelines on the bag but monitor individual energy needs. Growing Danes need ample calories and nutrition to thrive.

- Feed 2-3 meals a day until 6 months old, then consider dropping to twice daily. Keeping some meals prevents gorging.

- Use a slow feed bowl to prevent choking, bloating, and rapid eating. Raise food and water bowls.

- Avoid strenuous exercise 1 hour before and after eating to prevent dangerous gastric torsion.

- Limit play right after eating to calm activities like chews or training sessions - no high-energy play.

- Carefully monitor Great Dane puppy growth rates. Overnutrition leading to rapid growth can harm joint health. But undernutrition also impairs development.

- Unless overweight, most adult Danes can be fed free choice quality kibble available at all times. Monitor intake and adjust accordingly.

- Supplement dry kibble with some wet food, raw or homemade options for variety.

- Avoid over-treating. Stick to healthy options like fruits, vegetables, and lean meats.

Your Great Dane's diet can impact their lifelong health and comfort. Work closely with your veterinarian and research breed-specific nutritional guidelines.

Chapter Nine

Health and Care for Your Great Dane

Grooming and Coat Care

The short, smooth coat of a Great Dane takes minimal grooming effort:

- Brush your Great Dane weekly using a rubber curry brush or hound mitt to remove dead hair and spread skin oils.

- Bathe only when necessary with a gentle canine shampoo. Over-bathing strips protective oils. Spot clean dirty paws or other unclean areas between thorough baths.

- Trim nails carefully every 2-3 weeks until worn down naturally from activity on hard surfaces. Avoid cutting the quick. Introduce nail trims slowly with treats to foster cooperation.

- Inspect and clean face folds regularly on some Danes to prevent illness. Gently cleanse deep folds with a dry cloth or cleansing wipe.

- Brush teeth ideally daily using dog-safe toothpaste and finger brush. This avoids dental disease.

- Check and clean droopy ears at least regularly. Gently cleanse the inside folds with a cleansing wipe. Monitor for any redness or odor indicating infection.

- Use dog-safe dry shampoo or wet wipe to freshen the coat between thorough baths, especially on light-colored Danes where dirt shows.

- Provide a dog ramp or stairs for car access to avoid stressing joints by jumping down. Lift puppies till mature.

- Discourage jumping on persons or things. Carrying excess weight affects the developing bones and joints.

With weekly brushing and nail/ear care, the Great Dane's grooming needs are relatively easy overall. Maintain a healthy body state.

Recognizing Common Health Issues

Great Danes are prone to various genetic health issues owners should be aware of:

- Gastric dilatation volvulus or GDV is a life-threatening emergency where the stomach twists. Symptoms include fruitless retching, distention, and collapse. Seek immediate surgery if suspected.

- Cardiomyopathy is a frequent heart condition. Symptoms may include exercise intolerance, coughing, weakness, and fainting. Have cardiac examinations done routinely.

- Hip and elbow dysplasia – have OFA or PennHIP radiographs assessed for joint concerns prior to breeding. Monitor for lameness or stiffness.

- Hypothyroidism is a prevalent hormonal illness. Signs include coat difficulties, lethargy, obesity, and skin infections. Diagnose via bloodwork. Most dogs live well managed on thyroid medication.

- Allergies to dietary or environmental factors can cause chronic itching and ear/skin infections. Trial allergy elimination diets if chronic concerns emerge.

- Cancer is a leading cause of mortality for Danes. Owners should monitor for tumors, irregular bleeding or discharge, and other worrying indications. Catching it early substantially improves prognosis.

- Bloat - Don't allow strong activity or excessive water consumption right before or after meals. This contributes to deadly GDV risk.

Know the common concerns prone in the breed and catch problems early for optimum outcomes. Routine wellness examinations assist prevent or decrease health concerns.

Caring for a Senior Great Dane

Great Danes' shorter lifespans imply they attain senior status earlier than most breeds. Expect to make adjustments around age 6-8 years:

- Schedule wellness checks with blood work every 6 months to discover age-related disease early. Baseline senior bloodwork around age 6 is wise.

- Feed a good-grade senior dog food intended for big breeds. Watch bodily condition and adjust calories accordingly.

- Provide orthopedic beds and mobility aid harnesses/ramps if joint stiffness develops. Keep nails trimmed to minimize slipping on floors.

- Increase glucosamine/chondroitin and fish oil pills to help aging joints. Watch for limping, and problems standing.

- Adjust exercise to your senior Dane's needs - often shorter but more frequent walks to maintain mobility and prevent muscle atrophy.

- Monitor for lumps, bumps, or other physical changes and report to your veterinarian promptly. Cancer risk increases.

- Consider prescription urinary and digestive support foods if accidents happen or hunger drops. Routine age-related changes are prevalent.

- Spoil your senior Great Dane with their favorite activities and human attention. The end of life approaches too rapidly - make every day count.

- Prepare for characteristic senior Dane concerns like arthritis, cancer, and cardiac issues. Save funds for specialty veterinarian care as needed.

With diligent preventive care and high-quality nourishment, many Great Danes spend several good years as seniors before their time comes. Cherish this wonderful breed.

Chapter Ten

Enjoying Your Great Dane

Including Your Dog in Activities

One of the benefits of having a Great Dane is incorporating them into family activities. Consider these activity ideas:

- Visit new outdoor restaurants with dog-friendly patios. This combines dining out with socialization. Bring chews/toys to keep your Dane settled.

- Sign up for charity dog walks or fun runs. Great Danes make quite the impression! Just monitor for overheating on hot days.

- Take your Great Dane kayaking, tubing, or paddling if they are strong swimmers and enjoy the water. Have a dog life jacket and freshwater accessible.

- Go hiking together on lovely trails. Your Great Dane will love exploring the outdoors with you. Bring plenty of drinks and take rest breaks.

- Include your Dane when gardening. Let them curiously examine your work outdoors from their bed nearby.

- Bring your Great Dane shopping at hardware stores, tractor supply shops, and other dog-friendly retailers. It gets them socialized to new sights and sounds.

- Enter your Dane into a local dog show! Conformation and obedience trials are wonderful goals to train for.

- Have picnics, campouts, or beach days with your Great Dane. They'll appreciate joining family activities and mealtimes.

- Sign up for a training class like nose work or agility that provides mental stimulation and time together.

Great Danes really love participating in their family's busy lifestyle. Include them wherever it's safe and suitable.

Traveling with a Great Dane

With sufficient planning, Great Danes can handle travel:

- Invest in a huge robust container reinforced for crash protection to transport your Dane or utilize a strapped harness in the rear seat.

- Help kids adjust to automobile journeys by taking numerous short trips to enjoyable places like drive-through ice cream stores. Make it positive.

- Pack food, bowls, prescriptions, cleaning supplies, a favorite toy or blanket, leash, and other road trip requirements.

- Scout pet-friendly accommodations in advance. Ask about size restrictions, prices, and availability of grassy relief areas and walking pathways.

- Schedule veterinarian visits before major travel to get their health certified. Obtain health certifications if crossing state lines.

- Allow regular exercise stops during road journeys - don't leave your Great Dane locked in the car for more than 2-3 hours at a period.

- Ensure your Dane always wears identity tags in case they are lost. Consider microchipping as well.

- Never leave your Great Dane alone unattended in the car or get to your destination without confirmed pet policies. Avoid risks.

With proper work and packing, you and your Great Dane may have great experiences together! Travel safely.

Fun Tricks and Games

In addition to training, enjoy entertaining games with your Great Dane to improve your bond:

- Play moderate tug and fetch games using toys sized for big breeds to securely enjoy chewing and gripping development.

- Hide treats throughout the house and urge your Great Dane to hunt for them using their keen nose. Make them really sniff them out!

- Set up your Dane's kibble dinner in food puzzles, snuffle mats, plush Kongs, etc. to provide mental enrichment.

- Teach fun tricks like spinning, army crawling, closing doors, or picking up stuff on cue. Keep training sessions brief and lively.

- Fill a kiddie pool with toys and balls for your Great Dane to push around with their nose and paws. Add ice cubes too!

- Practice engaging nose work games uncovering hidden fragrant things. Great Danes excel at using their nose.

- Play "go find" utilizing family members - have your Great Dane sit/stay then go locate other people in your home.

- Try canine fitness equipment like tunnels, agility ramps, and fitness hurdles set up safely in your yard for energetic activities.

- Take hilarious images and videos of your Great Dane being their typical goofy self. Capture the amusing shenanigans.

Most importantly, lavish your Great Dane with love, pets, and quality time. That's the best reward of all!

Chapter Eleven

Great Dane-Specific Training Considerations

Training for Size and Strength

Great Danes' immense size and power demand appropriate training methods for success:

- Begin leash training as soon as feasible. Pulled by an adult Great Dane, most owners have difficulty maintaining control. Use front-clip harnesses and multiple clips below the neck as needed.

- Do NOT physically dominate or punish Great Dane puppies. This breeds fear and hostility when applied to big breeds. Always use positive encouragement.

- Reward DESIRED actions continually. Prevent problem behaviors by regulating the environment during training. Set your Dane up for success.

- Recognize size-related dangers such as stair climbing, heat intolerance, and overexertion. Adjust activities accordingly to avoid harm.

- Socialize extensively with new people, animals, and places starting early. A poorly socialized Great Dane signals danger due to their talents.

- Desensitize to handling, tests, and grooming frequently. Teach cooperation with touch to adult size. An unwanted gigantic breed is harmful.

- Target train touch cues on hand or target stick initially. Lure training prepares for future cue compliance.

- Respect personal space boundaries. Never back a Great Dane into a corner. Fear feels threatening when they are big.

- Help strangers approach safely. Ask owners before touching a Great Dane and have strangers offer goodies before touching.

- Prevent rehearsal of undesired leaping, mouthing, or harsh play. These habits become risky long-term. Manage their energy and behavior from the outset.

At every age, remember your Great Dane's capabilities. Tailor training to their genetic strengths like scent work, but also gently modify their behavior around suitable size-related restrictions. Patience and kindness achieve results.

Understanding the Gentle Giant: Temperament Insights

Great Danes are nicknamed "Gentle Giants" because of their sensitive, devoted natures. Understand major breed characteristics:

- Eager to Please: Great Danes bond strongly and seek to make their owners happy. Use this to motivate training.

- Sensitive: Harsh corrections overwhelm Danes. Train utilizing positive reinforcement and clear communication.

- Docile: Most Great Danes take handling, loud sounds, crowds, and other stimuli easily compared to many breeds when socialized appropriately.

- Aloof: Great Danes are selective and slower to warm up to new people compared to extreme "people dogs." Socialize broadly, but let them decide the pace.

- Intelligent: Great Danes learn rapidly and thrive when challenged cognitively. Teach advanced cues and tricks to suit their working breed inclinations.

- Dependent: More than other breeds, Great Danes demand intimate human interaction and participatory play. Involve them extensively in your daily lives and activities.

- Calm: Great Danes are easy going indoors and lack severe exercise needs. But they still demand regular walks and attention from their family.

- Stubborn: Great Danes selectively listen. Stay optimistic yet firm during training. Practice engagement and motivation using high-value rewards.

- Predictable: Well-raised Great Danes are steady and predictable in temperament from puppyhood forward thanks to meticulous breeding.

Knowing breed-specific qualities allows you to adapt training in a way that sets your Great Dane and you up for success via understanding.

Tailoring Training to Individual Personality

While Great Danes share basic breed features, individual variances contribute enormously to training:

- Confident Danes need higher difficulty in training and intensive socialization to prevent pushing boundaries.

- Shy Danes require gradual exposure to gain confidence and conquer fear through reward-based baby steps.

- Calmer Danes thrive on consistent schedules with appropriate exercise and play. Highly energetic Danes need more outlets for their energy.

- Independent Danes require motivation and engagement work. Velcro Danes calls for impulse control training.

- Faster learners succeed with enhanced training games and signals. Slower learners require more repetition for habits to stick.

- Excitable Danes respond better to training following hard exercises to take the edge off. Lower-energy Danes need mental stimulation to focus.

- Danes with a high predatory drive must learn strong "leave it" messages around tiny animals. More docile Danes emphasize training on interaction.

- Noise-sensitive Danes require gradual desensitization sessions utilizing recordings and treats. Bombproof Danes can be exposed to new sights and sounds freely.

The value of considering your Great Dane as an individual cannot be stressed. Evaluate their distinctive characteristics and alter your training approach accordingly. Be flexible and you'll be rewarded with a joyful, well-mannered companion best suited to your lifestyle.

20 homemade food recipes ideas for great dane with ingredients and preparation instructions

1. Beef and Sweet Potato Stew

Ingredients:

- 2 pounds lean ground beef
- 2 sweet potatoes, peeled and diced
- 1 cup green beans, chopped
- 4 cups beef broth

Instructions:

1. Brown ground beef in a big pot.

2. Add diced sweet potatoes, chopped green beans, and beef broth.

3. Simmer until vegetables are soft and the stew thickens.

2. Chicken and Brown Rice Casserole

Ingredients:
- 3 cups cooked chicken, shredded
- 2 cups brown rice, cooked
- 1 cup carrots, grated
- 1/2 cup peas

Instructions:
1. Mix shredded chicken, cooked brown rice, grated carrots, and peas.
2. Spread the mixture in a casserole dish.
3. Bake at 350°F (175°C) for 25-30 minutes until golden brown.

3. Salmon and Quinoa Delight

Ingredients:
- 2 cups cooked salmon, flakes

- 1 cup quinoa, cooked
- 1/2 cup spinach, coarsely chopped
- 1 tablespoon fish oil

Instructions:

1. Combine flaked salmon, cooked quinoa, and chopped spinach.
2. Drizzle with fish oil and combine well.
3. Serve at room temperature.

4. Turkey and Pumpkin Stew

Ingredients:
- 1.5 pounds ground turkey
- 1 cup pumpkin puree
- 1/2 cup blueberries
- 1 tablespoon olive oil

Instructions:

1. Cook ground turkey till browned.
2. Mix in pumpkin puree, blueberries, and olive oil.

3. Simmer until the stew acquires a hearty consistency.

5. Lamb and Barley Bowl

Ingredients:

- 2 cups lamb, cooked and diced

- 1 cup barley, cooked

- 1/2 cup carrots, finely chopped

- 1 tablespoon coconut oil

Instructions:

1. Combine diced lamb, cooked barley, and chopped carrots.

2. Add melted coconut oil and mix completely.

3. Allow the mixture to cool before serving.

6. Venison and Sweet Potato Casserole

Ingredients:

- 1.5 pounds venison, cooked and shredded

- 2 sweet potatoes, peeled and thinly sliced

- 1 cup broccoli florets

- 1 cup beef broth

Instructions:

1. Shred cooked venison and put it in a casserole dish.

2. Add thinly sliced sweet potatoes and broccoli.

3. Pour beef broth over the layers and bake until the sweet potatoes are cooked.

7. Turkey and Blueberry Biscuits

Ingredients:

- 2 cups ground turkey, cooked

- 1 cup blueberries

- 1 cup oats

- 1 egg

Instructions:

1. Mix ground turkey, blueberries, oats, and beaten egg.

2. Form the ingredients into biscuits and lay them on a baking pan.

3. Bake at 350°F (175°C) for 15-20 minutes until golden brown.

8. Duck and Pea Risotto

Ingredients:

- 1 cup duck meat, cooked and diced
- 1 cup peas
- 1 cup brown rice, cooked
- 1 tablespoon olive oil

Instructions:

1. Sauté diced duck meat and peas in olive oil.

2. Add cooked brown rice and stir until fully blended.

3. Allow it to cool before serving.

9. Chicken Liver with Potato Mash

Ingredients:

- 2 cups chicken liver, cooked and mashed

- 1 cup potatoes, boiled and mashed

- 1/2 cup green beans, coarsely chopped

- 1 tablespoon fish oil

Instructions:

1. Mash cooked chicken liver and potatoes together.

2. Add finely chopped green beans and fish oil.

3. Serve at room temperature.

10. Pork and Apple Oatmeal Bowl

Ingredients:

- 1 cup pork, cooked and diced

- 1 apple, grated

- 1/2 cup oats, boiled

- 1 tablespoon coconut oil

Instructions:

1. Mix diced pork, grated apple, and cooked oats.

2. Incorporate melted coconut oil and mix completely.

3. Allow it to cool before presenting to your Great Dane.

11. Salmon and Pumpkin Bites

Ingredients:
- 1.5 cups cooked salmon, flaked
- 1 cup pumpkin, diced
- 1/4 cup parsley, coarsely chopped
- 1 tablespoon olive oil

Instructions:
1. Mix flaked fish, diced pumpkin, and minced parsley.
2. Form the mixture into bite-sized balls.
3. Drizzle with olive oil and serve chilled.

12. Venison and Carrot Stew

Ingredients:
- 1.5 pounds venison, cooked and shredded
- 1 cup carrots, sliced

- 1 cup green peas
- 1 cup beef broth

Instructions:

1. Shred cooked venison and place it in a pot.

2. Add sliced carrots, green peas, and beef broth.

3. Simmer until vegetables are soft and the stew thickens.

13. Quail and Spinach Casserole

Ingredients:
- 1 cup quail meat, cooked and chopped
- 1/2 cup spinach, finely chopped
- 1/4 cup carrots, grated
- 1 tablespoon fish oil

Instructions:

1. Combine chopped quail, chopped spinach, and grated carrots.

2. Add fish oil and stir well.

3. Serve at room temperature.

14. Lamb and Broccoli Omelette

Ingredients:

- 1 cup lamb, cooked and diced

- 3 eggs

- 1 cup broccoli, chopped

- 1 tablespoon coconut oil

Instructions:

1. Cook diced lamb in coconut oil.

2. Whisk eggs and pour them over the lamb.

3. Add chopped broccoli, heat until set, and serve.

15. Sardine and Zucchini Medley

Ingredients:

- 1 can of sardines in water, drained

- 1 cup zucchini, sliced

- 1/4 cup blueberries

- 1 tablespoon olive oil

Instructions:

1. Mash drained sardines and add with cut zucchini.

2. Add blueberries and olive oil, and stir thoroughly.

3. Serve at room temperature.

16. Turkey and Cranberry Muffins

Ingredients:

- 2 cups ground turkey, cooked

- 1 cup cranberries, chopped

- 1 cup oats

- 1 egg

Instructions:

1. Mix ground turkey, chopped cranberries, oats, and beaten egg.

2. Spoon the mixture into muffin pans.

3. Bake at 350°F (175°C) for 20-25 minutes.

17. Duck and Apple Bites

Ingredients:

- 1 cup duck meat, boiled and shredded

- 1 apple, grated

- 1/4 cup parsley, coarsely chopped

- 1 tablespoon fish oil

Instructions:

1. Combine shredded duck, grated apple, and minced parsley.

2. Form the mixture into bite-sized balls.

3. Drizzle with fish oil and serve chilled.

18. Chicken and Green Bean Stir-Fry

Ingredients:

- 2 cups cooked chicken, diced

- 1 cup green beans, sliced

- 1 cup brown rice, cooked

- 1 tablespoon soy sauce

Instructions:

1. Sauté diced chicken and sliced green beans.

2. Add cooked brown rice and soy sauce, and mix thoroughly.

3. Allow it to cool before serving.

19. Salmon and Cauliflower Mash

Ingredients:

- 1.5 cups cooked salmon, flaked
- 1 cup cauliflower, boiled and mashed
- 1/4 cup carrots, finely chopped
- 1 tablespoon olive oil

Instructions:

1. Mix flaked salmon, mashed cauliflower, and diced carrots.

2. Drizzle with olive oil and mix completely.

3. Serve at room temperature.

20. Pork and Sweet Potato Medley

Ingredients:

- 1 cup pork, cooked and diced

- 1 sweet potato, peeled and diced

- 1/2 cup peas

- 1 tablespoon coconut oil

Instructions:

1. Sauté diced pork, diced sweet potato, and peas in coconut oil.

2. Allow it to cool before serving it to your Great Dane.

www.ingramcontent.com/pod-product-compliance
Lightning Source LLC
Chambersburg PA
CBHW070817260726

48660CB00005B/1883